8.25

Arranged for all portable keyboards *by Kenneth Baker.*

THE COMPLETE KEYBOARD PLAYER

SONGBOOK 8

Wise Publications
London/New York/Sydney

Exclusive distributors:
Music Sales Limited
8/9 Frith Street, London, W1V 5TZ, England
Music Sales Pty. Limited
120 Rothschild Avenue, Rosebery, NSW 2018, Australia

This book © Copyright 1990 by
Wise Publications
Order No. AM78981
UK ISBN 0.7119.2187.3

Designed by Pearce Marchbank Studio
Arranged by Kenneth Baker
Compiled by Peter Evans
Music processed by Musicprint

Music Sales' complete catalogue lists thousands of titles and is
free from your local music book shop, or direct from Music Sales Limited.
Please send a cheque/postal order for £1.50 for postage to Music Sales Limited,
Newmarket Road, Bury St Edmunds, Suffolk IP33 3YB.

UNCHAINED MELODY

Music by Alex North
Words by Hy Zaret

Suggested registration: string ensemble
Rhythm: bossa nova
Tempo: medium (♩ = 116)

Oh, my love, my dar - ling, I've
Time goes by so slow - ly, and

mp

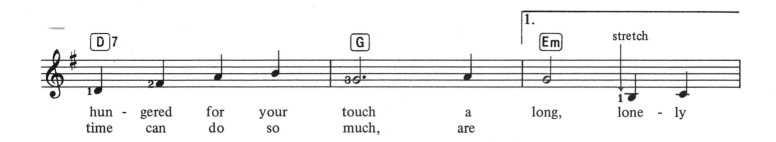

hun - gered for your touch a long, lone - ly
time can do so much, are

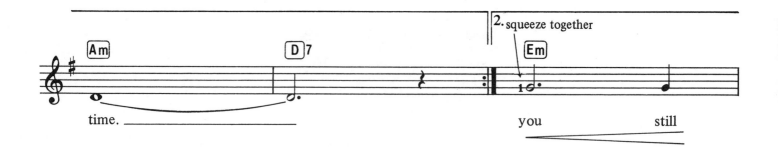

time. _____ you still

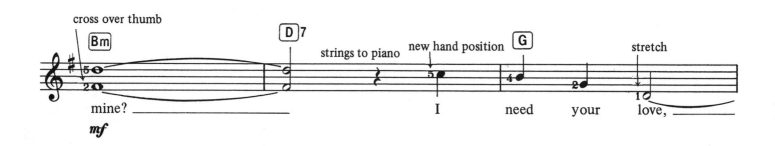

mine? _____ I need your love, _____

mf

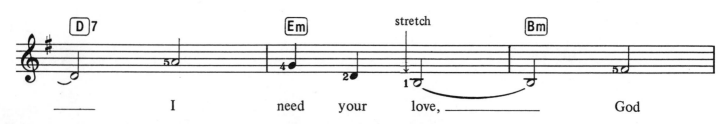

_____ I need your love, _____ God

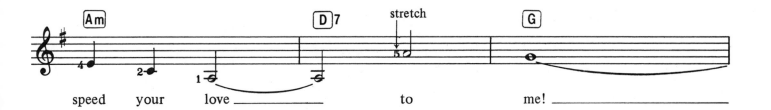

speed your love _____ to me! _____

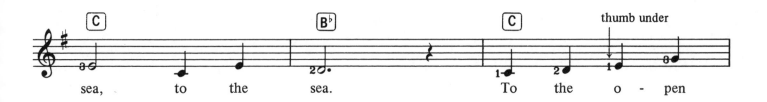

piano to strings

(FINE)

Lone - ly ri - vers flow to the

p

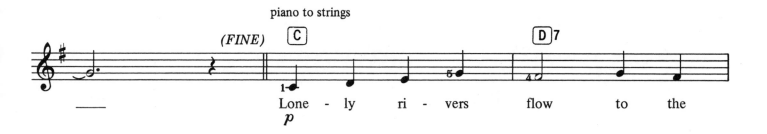

sea, to the sea. To the o - pen

thumb under

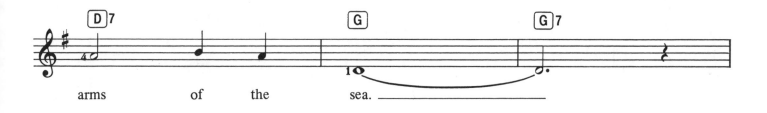

arms of the sea. _____

Lone - ly ri - vers sigh: "Wait for me, wait for me!"

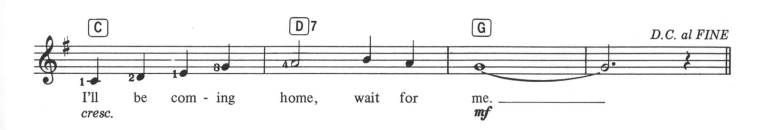

D.C. al FINE

I'll be com - ing home, wait for me. _____

cresc. *mf*

LOVE'S BEEN GOOD TO ME

Words & Music by Rod McKuen

Suggested registration: clarinet
Rhythm: bossa nova
Tempo: medium (♩ = 96)

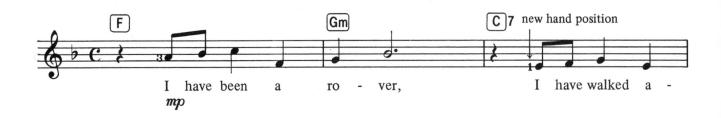

I have been a ro - ver, I have walked a -

lone. Hiked a hun - dred high - ways,

ne - ver found a home. Still in all I'm

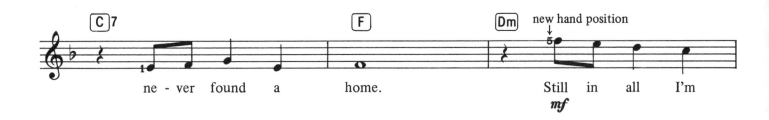

hap - py, the rea - son is, you see:

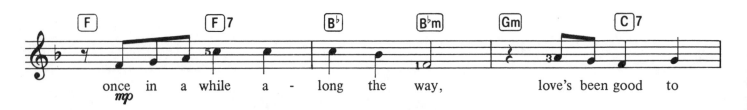

once in a while a - long the way, love's been good to

me. There was a girl in Den - ver,

be - fore the sum - mer storm. Oh, her arms were

ten - der! Oh! her arms were warm! And she could

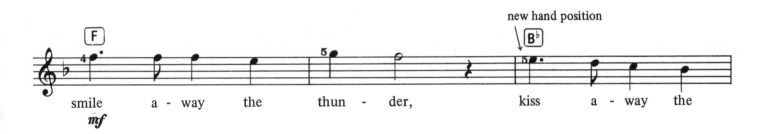

smile a - way the thun - der, kiss a - way the
mf

rain. And ev - en though she's gone a - way,
mp

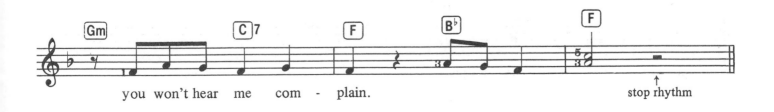

you won't hear me com - plain. stop rhythm

7

CAROLINA MOON

Words by Benny Davis
Music by Joe Burke

Suggested registration: flute
Rhythm: waltz
Tempo: fairly slow (♩ = 84)

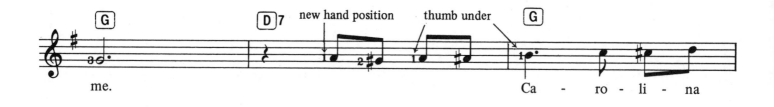

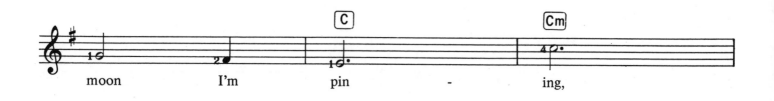

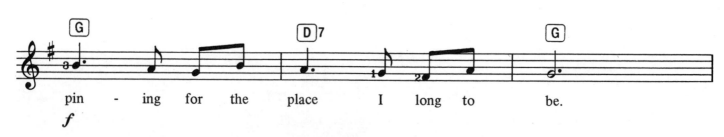

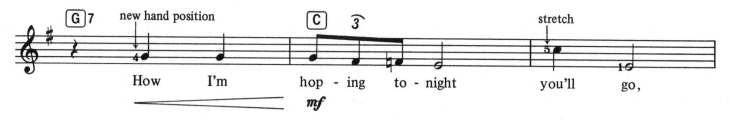

How I'm hop - ing to - night you'll go,

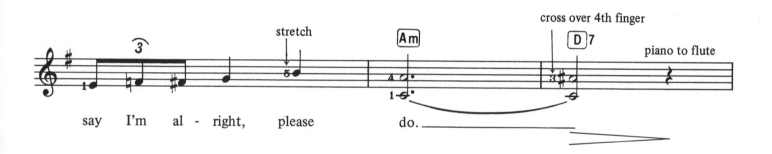

go to the right win - dow, scat - ter your light,

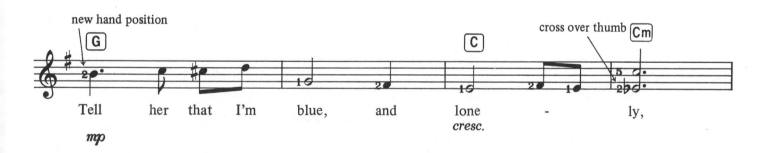

say I'm al - right, please do.

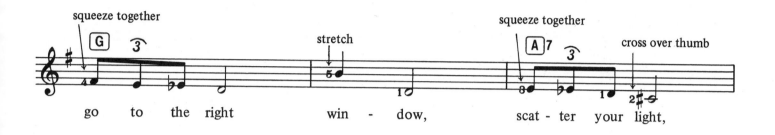

Tell her that I'm blue, and lone - ly,

dream - y Ca - ro - li - na moon.

ARRIVEDERCI ROMA

Words by Garinei & Giovannini/English Lyrics by Carl Sigman
Music by Renato Rascel

Suggested registration: mandolin
Rhythm: beguine (or bossa nova)
Tempo: medium (♩ = 104)

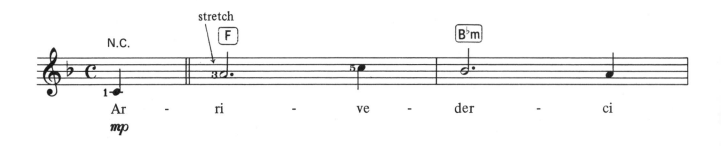

Ar - ri - ve - der - ci

Ro - ma. _____ Good bye, good -

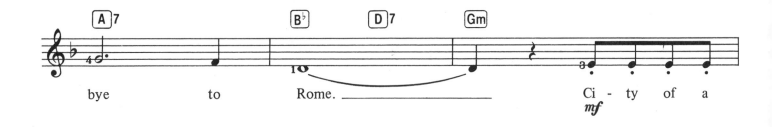

bye to Rome. _____ Ci - ty of a

mil - lion moon - lit pla - ces, ci - ty of a mil - lion warm em -

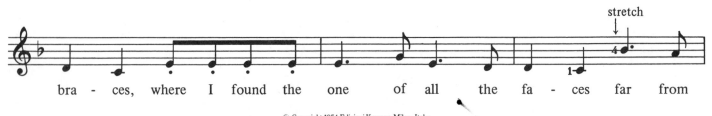

bra - ces, where I found the one of all the fa - ces far from

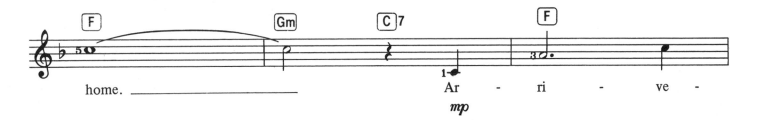

home. _____ Ar - ri - ve -

mp

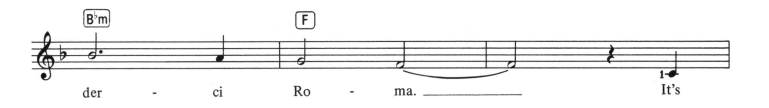

der - ci Ro - ma. _____ It's

time for us to part. _____

Save the wed-ding bells for my re - turn - ing, keep my lov - er's

mf

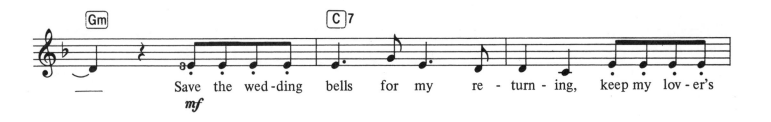

arms out-stretched and yearn - ing, please be sure the flame of love keeps

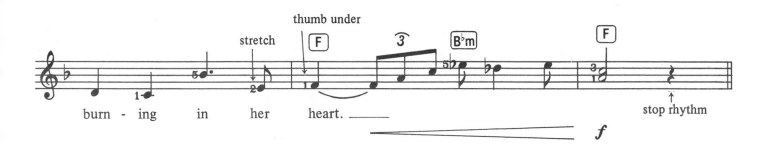

burn - ing in her heart. _____

f

I GOT IT BAD AND THAT AIN'T GOOD

Words & Music by Paul Webster & Duke Ellington

Suggested registration: saxophone
Rhythm: swing
Tempo: slow (♩ = 76)

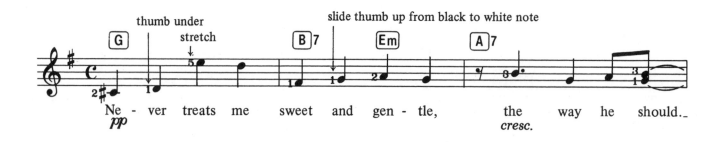

Ne - ver treats me sweet and gen - tle, the way he should.

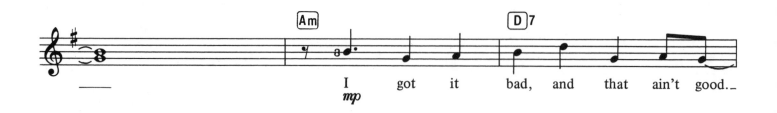

I got it bad, and that ain't good.

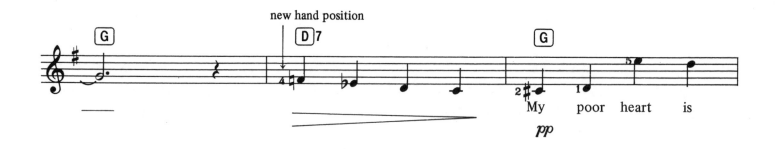

My poor heart is

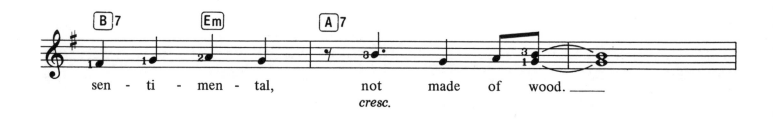

sen - ti - men - tal, not made of wood.

I got it bad and that ain't good.

saxophone to vibes

But when the week - end's o - ver, and

thumb under

Mon - day rolls a - roun', _____ I end up like I

cresc.

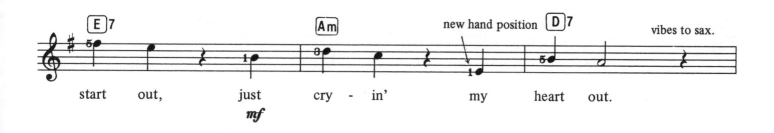

new hand position

vibes to sax.

start out, just cry - in' my heart out.

mf

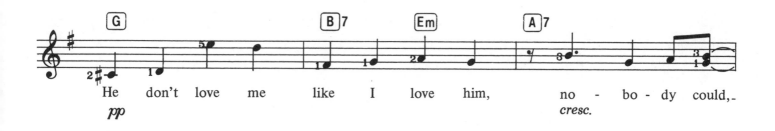

He don't love me like I love him, no - bo - dy could,_

pp

cresc.

I got it bad, and that ain't good._

mp

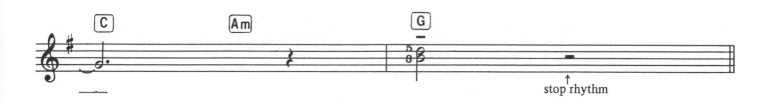

stop rhythm

_____

DIAMONDS ARE A GIRL'S BEST FRIEND

Words by Leo Robin
Music by Jule Styne

Suggested registration: trumpet
Rhythm: swing
Tempo: fast (♩ = 200)

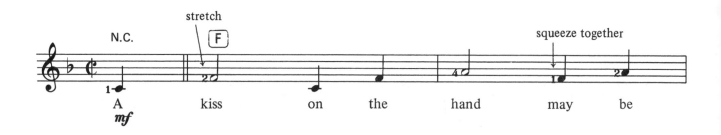

A kiss on the hand may be

quite con - ti - nen - tal, but dia - monds are a

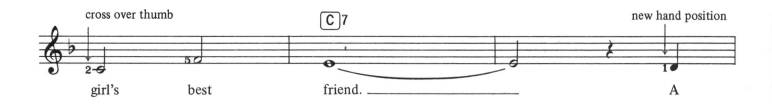

girl's best friend. _____ A

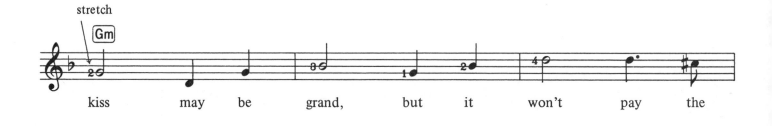

kiss may be grand, but it won't pay the

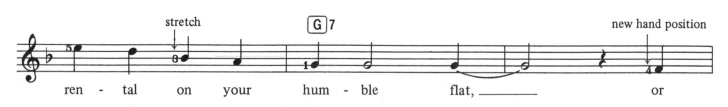

ren - tal on your hum - ble flat, _____ or

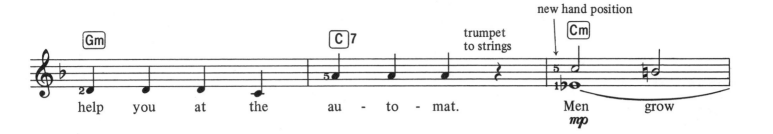

help you at the au - to - mat. Men grow

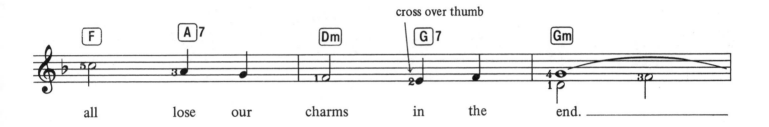

cold as girls grow old, and we

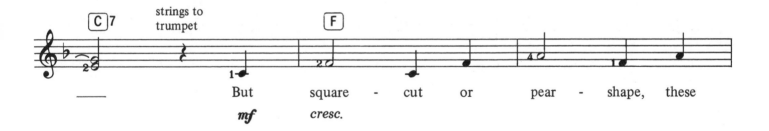

all lose our charms in the end.

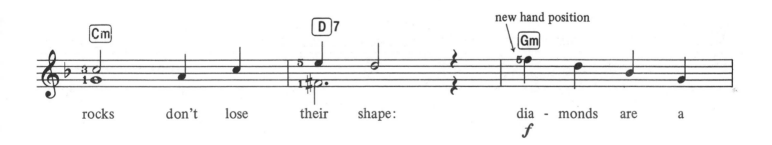

But square - cut or pear - shape, these

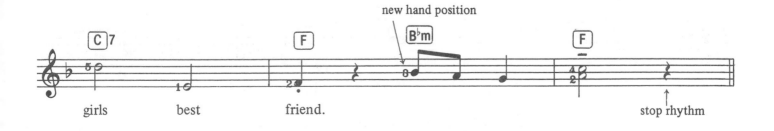

rocks don't lose their shape: dia - monds are a

girls best friend.

SMOKE GETS IN YOUR EYES

Music by Jerome Kern
Words by Otto Harbach

Suggested registration: piano
Rhythm: rhumba
Tempo: medium (♩ = 100)

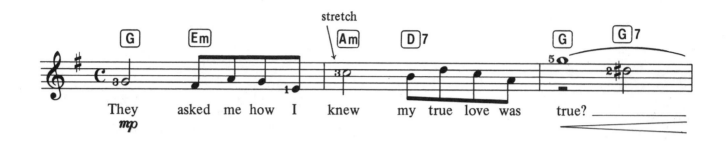

They asked me how I knew my true love was true? ___

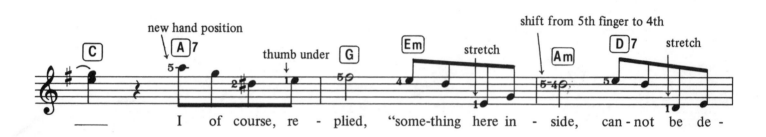

___ I of course, re - plied, "some-thing here in - side, can - not be de -

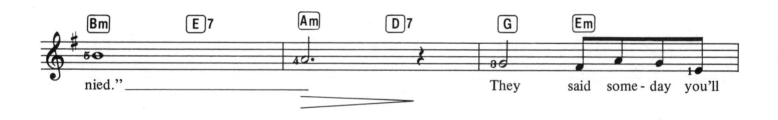

nied." ___ They said some - day you'll

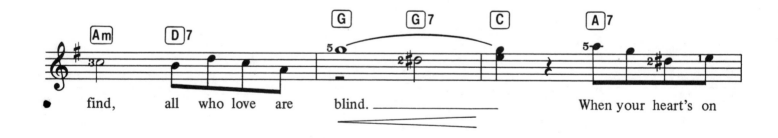

find, all who love are blind. ___ When your heart's on

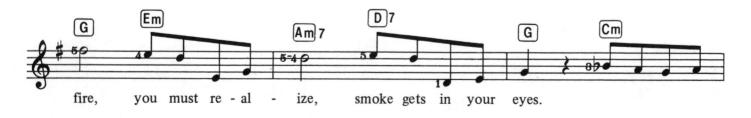

fire, you must re - al - ize, smoke gets in your eyes.

So I chaffed __ them and I gai - ly laughed __ to think they could

mf

doubt my love. Yet to - day ___ my love has

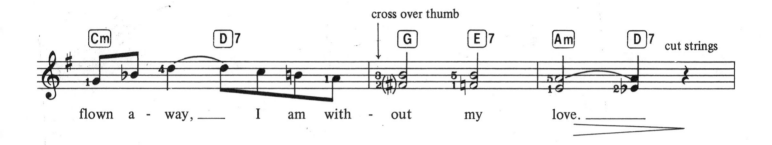

flown a - way, ___ I am with - out my love. ___

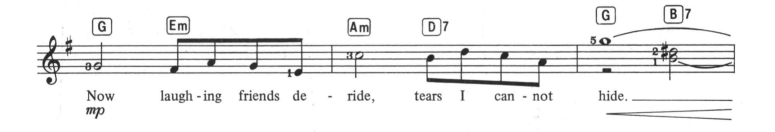

Now laugh - ing friends de - ride, tears I can - not hide. ___

mp

__ So I smile and say "when a love - ly flame dies, smoke gets in your

eyes." *p* stop rhythm

IT'S ALL IN THE GAME

Words by Carl Sigman
Music by Charles G. Dawes

Suggested registration: oboe
Rhythm: waltz
Tempo: medium (♩ = 84)

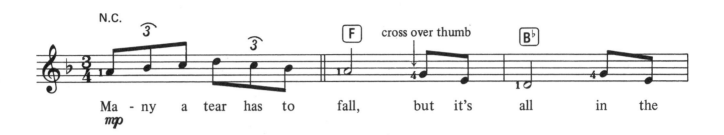

Ma - ny a tear has to fall, but it's all in the

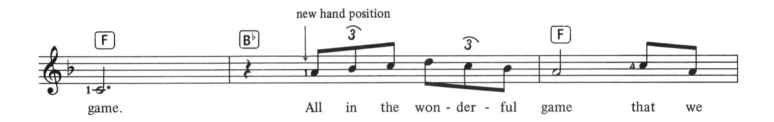

game. All in the won-der-ful game that we

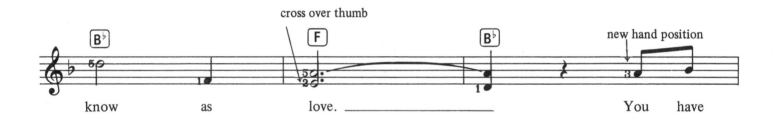

know as love. _____ You have

words with him, and your fu - ture's look - ing

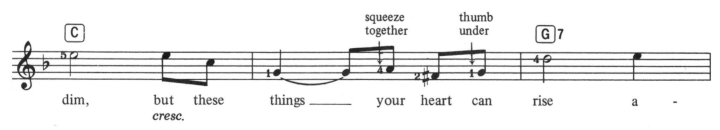

dim, but these things _____ your heart can rise a -

bove.

mf

Once in a while he won't call, but it's

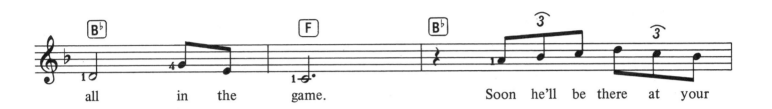

all in the game.

Soon he'll be there at your

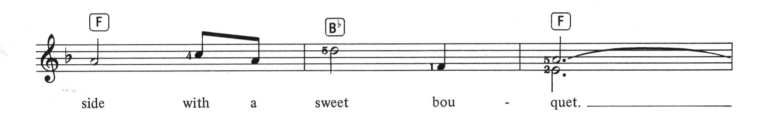

side with a sweet bou - quet. _____

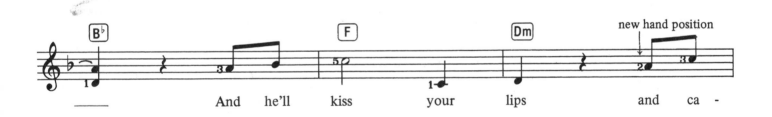

_____ And he'll kiss your lips and ca -

ress your wait - ing fin - ger - tips,

cresc.   *mf*

and your hearts will

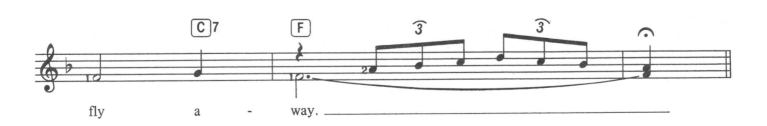

fly a - way. _____

I CAN'T GIVE YOU ANYTHING BUT LOVE

Words by Dorothy Fields
Music by Jimmy McHugh

Suggested registration: brass ensemble
Rhythm: swing
Tempo: quite fast (♩ = 152)

I can't give you an-y-thing but love,

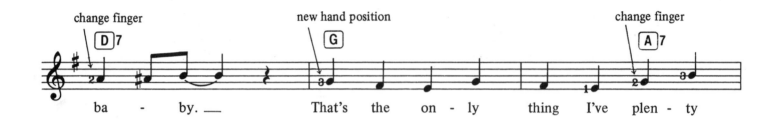

ba - by. ___ That's the on - ly thing I've plen - ty

of, ba - by. ___ Dream a - while, ___

scheme a - while, ___ we're sure to find

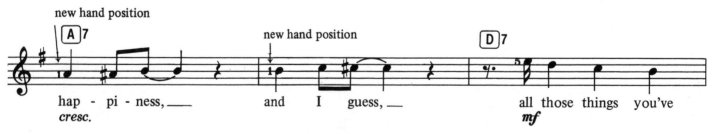

hap - pi - ness, ___ and I guess, ___ all those things you've

al - ways pined for. Gee, I'd like to see you look - ing

swell, ba - by. ___ Dia - mond brace - lets

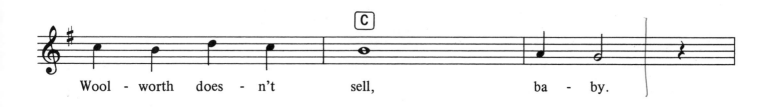

Wool - worth does - n't sell, ba - by.

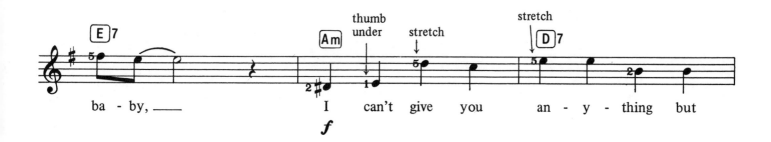

Till that luck - y day, you know darned well,

cresc.

ba - by, ___ I can't give you an - y - thing but

f

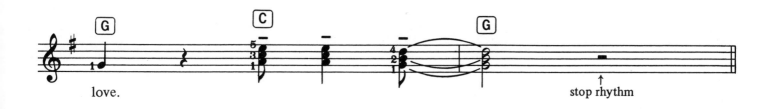

love. stop rhythm

21

DIDN'T WE?

Words & Music by Jim Webb

Suggested registration: guitar
Rhythm: bossa nova
Tempo: slow (♩ = 80)

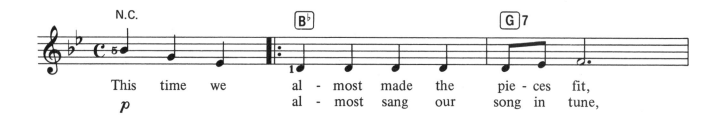

This time we al - most made the pie - ces fit,
p
al - most sang our song in tune,

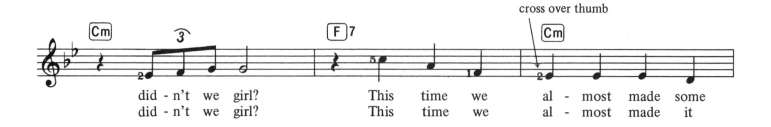

cross over thumb

did - n't we girl? This time we al - most made some
did - n't we girl? This time we al - most made it

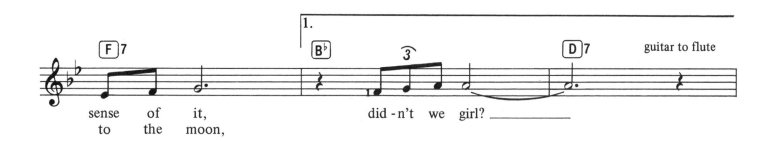

1.
guitar to flute

sense of it, did - n't we girl? ____
to the moon,

This time I had the ans - wer right here in hand, ____
cresc.

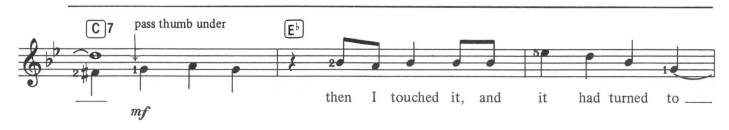

pass thumb under

then I touched it, and it had turned to ____
mf

sand. _____ This time we *mp* oh, did-n't we

girl? _____ This time we al-most made our *cresc.*

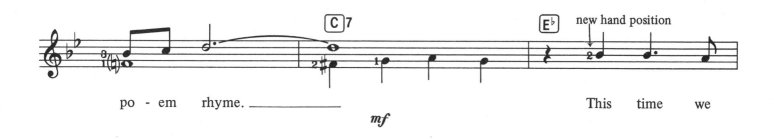

po - em rhyme. _____ *mf* This time we

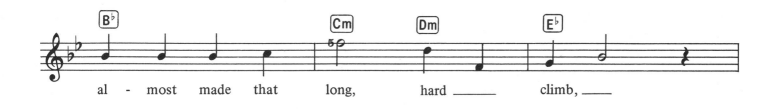

al — most made that long, hard _____ climb, _____

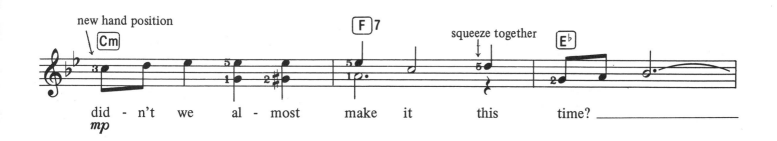

did - n't we al-most make it this time? _____ *mp*

CARAVAN

By Duke Ellington, Irving Mills & Juan Tizol

Suggested registration: saxophone
Rhythm: latin (eg: samba, mambo)
Tempo: fast (♩ = 120)

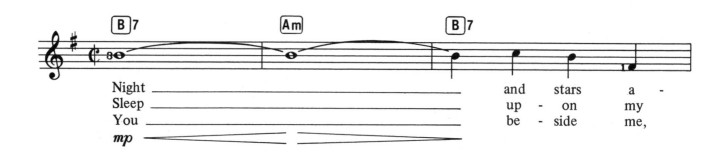

Night _____ and stars a -
Sleep _____ up - on my
You _____ be - side me,
mp

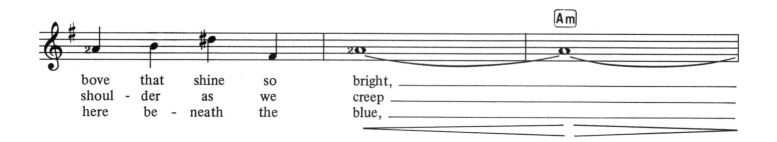

bove that shine so bright, _____
shoul - der as we creep _____
here be - neath the blue, _____

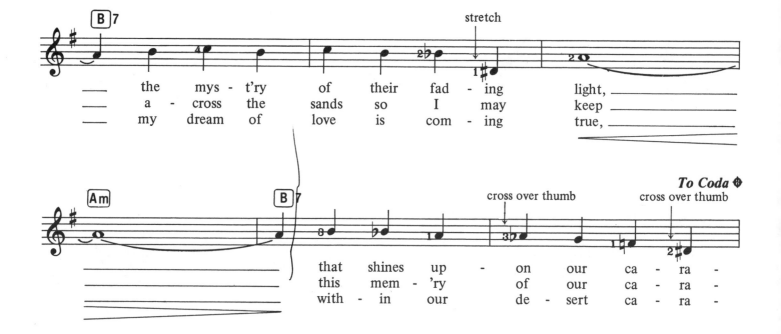

stretch

____ the mys - t'ry of their fad - ing light, _____
____ a - cross the sands so I may keep _____
____ my dream of love is com - ing true, _____

To Coda ⊕

cross over thumb   cross over thumb

that shines up - on our ca - ra -
this mem - 'ry of our ca - ra -
with - in our de - sert ca - ra -

(optional)

van. _____
van. _____

INSTRUMENTAL

Brass ensemble

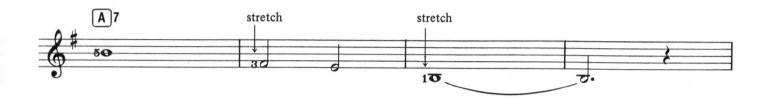

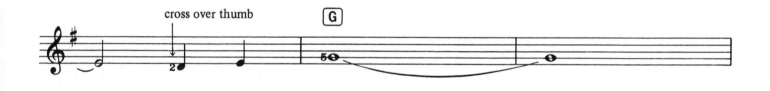

WHISPERING GRASS

Words by Fred Fisher
Music by Doris Fisher

Suggested registration: brass ensemble
Rhythm: shuffle (or swing)
Tempo: medium (♩ = 80)

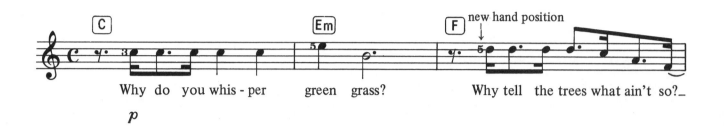

Why do you whis-per green grass? Why tell the trees what ain't so?

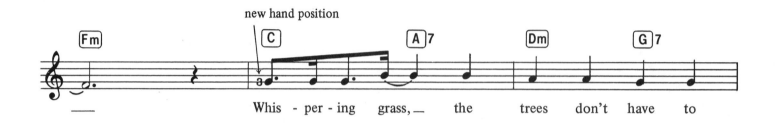

Whis-per-ing grass, the trees don't have to

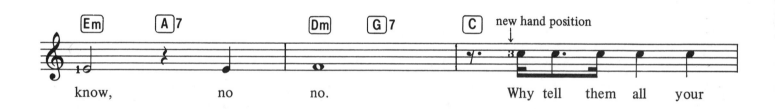

know, no no. Why tell them all your

se - crets? Who kiss'd her there long a - go.

Whis-per-ing grass, the trees don't need to know.

Don't you tell it to the breeze, 'cause she will tell the birds and bees and

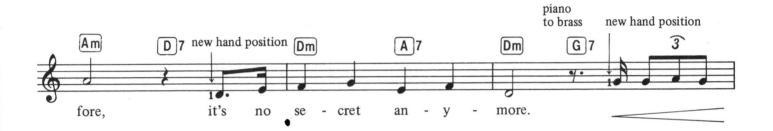

ev - 'ry - one will know, be-cause you told the blab-'ring trees, yes you told them once be -

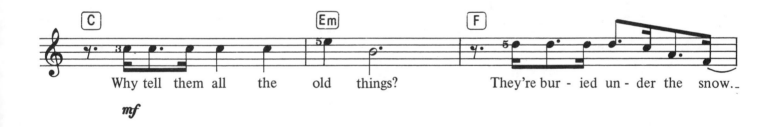

fore, it's no se - cret an - y - more.

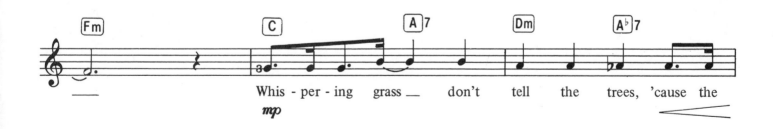

Why tell them all the old things? They're bur - ied un - der the snow.

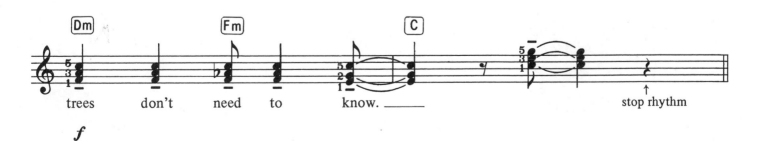

Whis - per - ing grass don't tell the trees, 'cause the

trees don't need to know.

THE DONKEY SERENADE

Words by Bob Wright & Chet Forrest
Music by Rudolf Friml & Herbert Stothart

Suggested registration: string ensemble
Rhythm: rhumba
Tempo: fairly fast (♩ = 132)

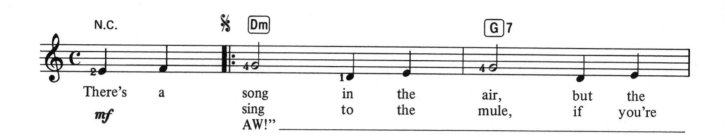

There's a song in the air, but the
sing to the air, mule, if you're
AW!"

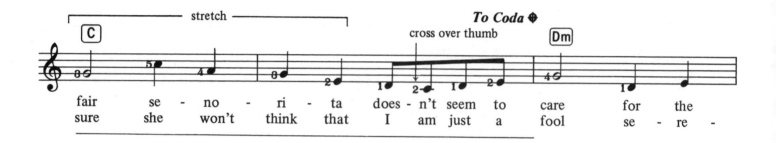

stretch   *To Coda* ✛

cross over thumb

fair se - no - ri - ta does - n't seem to care for the
sure she won't think that I am just a fool se - re -

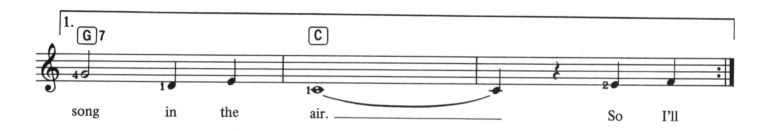

1.

song in the air. So I'll

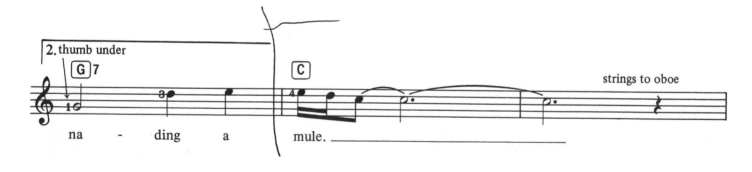

2. thumb under

strings to oboe

na - ding a mule.

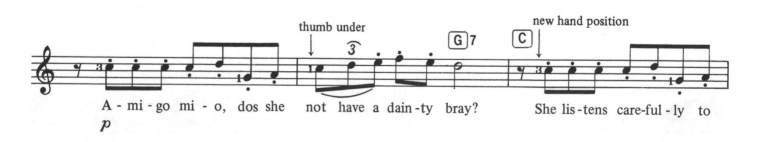

thumb under   new hand position

A - mi - go mi - o, dos she not have a dain - ty bray? She lis - tens care - ful - ly to

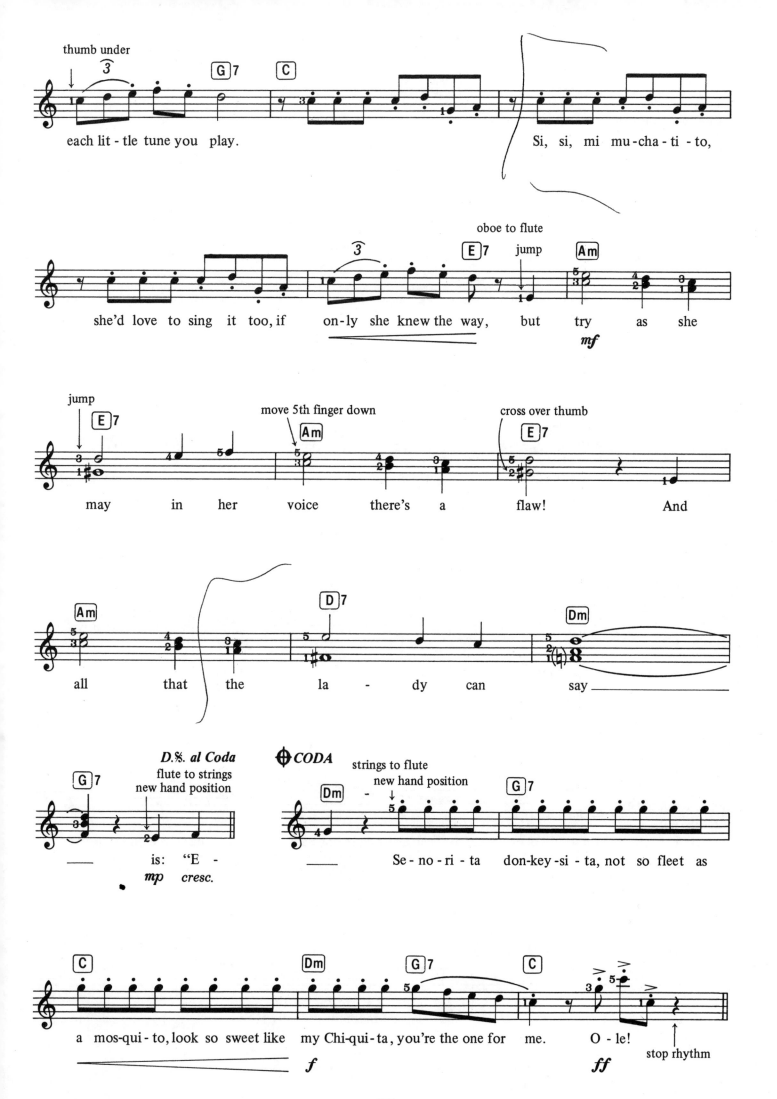

each lit - tle tune you play.

Si, si, mi mu - cha - ti - to,

she'd love to sing it too, if on - ly she knew the way, but try as she

may in her voice there's a flaw! And

all that the la - dy can say

is: "E -

Se - no - ri - ta don-key - si - ta, not so fleet as

a mos-qui - to, look so sweet like my Chi-qui - ta, you're the one for me. O - le!

POLKA DOTS AND MOONBEAMS

Words by Johnny Burke
Music by Jimmy Van Heusen

Suggested registration: trombone
Rhythm: bossa nova
Tempo: medium (♩ = 92)

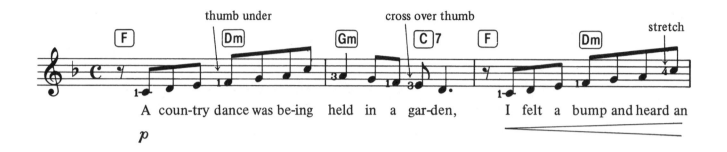

A coun-try dance was be-ing held in a gar-den, I felt a bump and heard an

"Oh, beg your par-don." Sud-den-ly I saw pol - ka dots and moon-beams

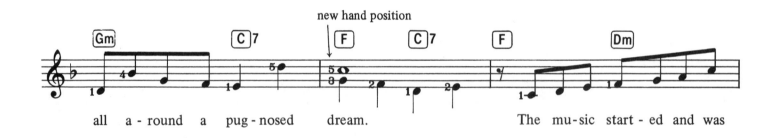

all a - round a pug - nosed dream. The mu-sic start - ed and was

I the per-plexed one, I held my breath and said "May I have the next one."

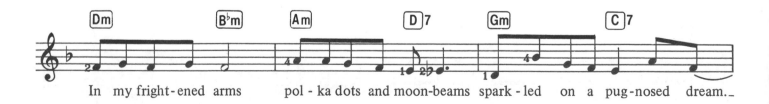

In my fright-ened arms pol - ka dots and moon-beams spark - led on a pug-nosed dream.

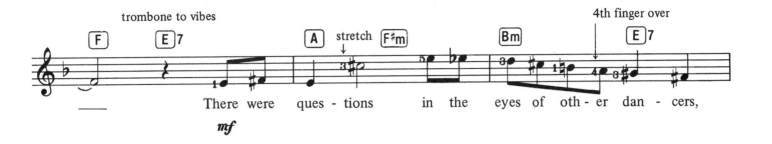

There were ques - tions in the eyes of oth - er dan - cers,

mf

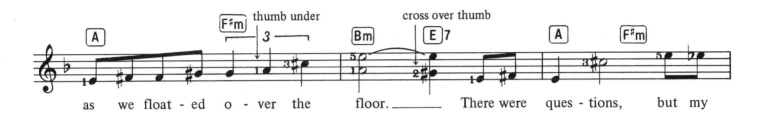

as we float - ed o - ver the floor._____ There were ques - tions, but my

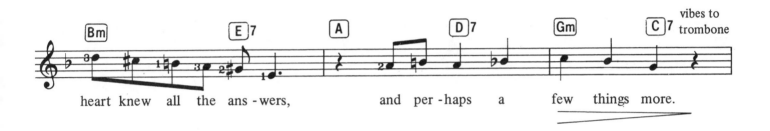

heart knew all the ans - wers, and per - haps a few things more.

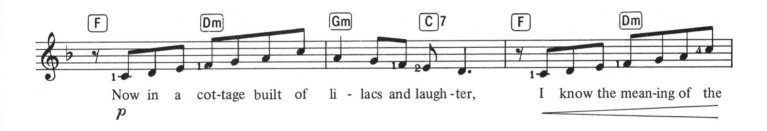

Now in a cot - tage built of li - lacs and laugh - ter, I know the mean - ing of the

p

words "ev - er af - ter." And I'll al - ways see pol - ka dots and moon-beams,

when I kiss the pug - nosed dream._____

HERNANDO'S HIDEAWAY

Words & Music by Richard Adler & Jerry Ross

Suggested registration: accordion
Rhythm: tango
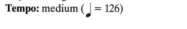

I know a dark se - clu - ded place, a place where no - one
All you see are sil - hou - ettes, and all you hear are

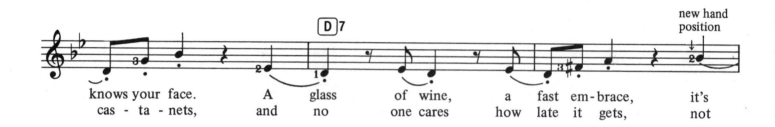

knows your face. A glass of wine, a fast em - brace, it's
cas - ta - nets, and no one cares how late it gets, not

called Her - nan - do's Hide - a - way! O - lay!
at Her - nan - do's Hide - a- - way! O - lay!

At the Gold - en Fin - ger Bowl, or

an - y place you go.

change finger

Gm   G7

You'll meet your Un-cle Max and   ev-'ry-one you know.

p   *mf*

Cm   jump   jump

If   you   go   to   the spot that   I   am think-in'   of,   *mf*

tuck 5th finger 'round 4th   jump up

A7   D7

you will   be free,   to gaze at me,   and talk   of

f

love!   Just   knock   three times   and   whis-per low,   that

mp

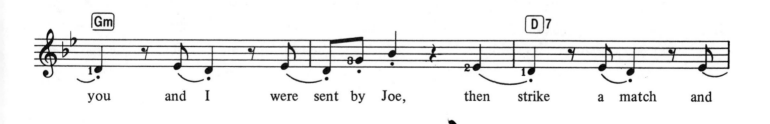

Gm   D7

you   and   I   were sent by Joe,   then   strike   a match   and

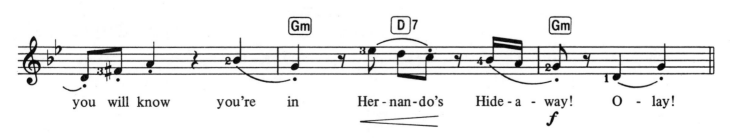

Gm   D7   Gm

you   will know   you're   in   Her-nan-do's   Hide-a-way!   O-lay!

f

SEND IN THE CLOWNS

Words & Music by Stephen Sondheim

Suggested registration: oboe (arpeggio if available)
Rhythm: slow rock
Tempo: slow (♩. = 54)

Is - n't it rich? _____ Are we a pair? Me here at
bliss? _____ Don't you ap - prove? One who keeps

last on the ground, you in mid - air. Send in the clowns. _____
tear - ing a round, one who can't move. Where are the

_____ Is - n't it clowns? Send in the clowns. Just when I'd

stopped _____ o - pen - ing doors. _____ Fi - nal - ly know - ing the one _____ that I want - ed was

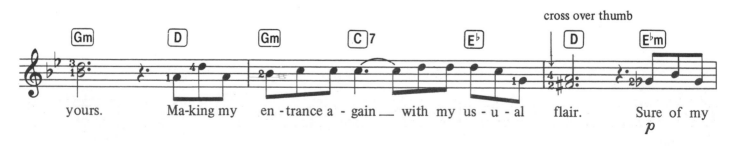

yours. Ma - king my en - trance a - gain _____ with my us - u - al flair. Sure of my

lines, _____ no - one is there. _____ Don't you love

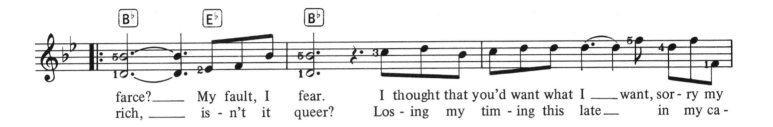

farce?_____ My fault, I fear.   I thought that you'd want what I ___ want, sor - ry my
rich, _____ is - n't it queer?   Los - ing my tim - ing this late___ in my ca -

dear.   But where are the clowns?   Quick, send in the
reer?   And where are the clowns?   There ought to be

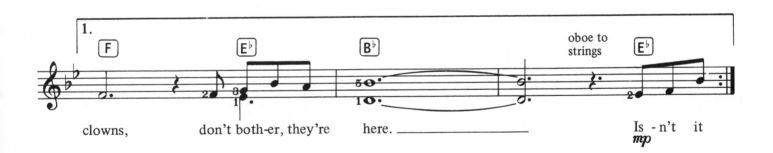

1.

clowns,   don't both-er, they're here. _____ Is - n't it
mp

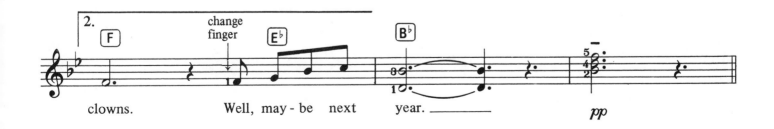

2.

clowns.   Well, may - be next year. _____ *pp*

COPACABANA

Words & Music by Al Stillman, Joao & Alberto Ribeiro

Suggested registration: accordion
Rhythm: samba
Tempo: fast (♩ = 208)

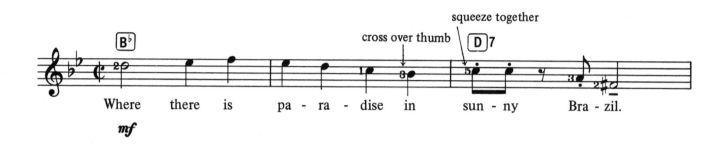

Where there is pa - ra - dise in sun - ny Bra - zil.

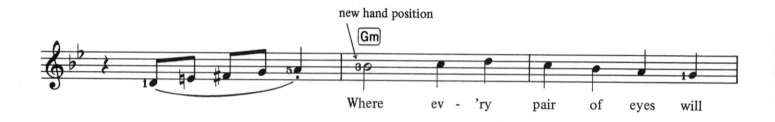

Where ev - 'ry pair of eyes will

give you a thrill Ask an - y

gay ro - man - cer, he will give you just one ans - wer,

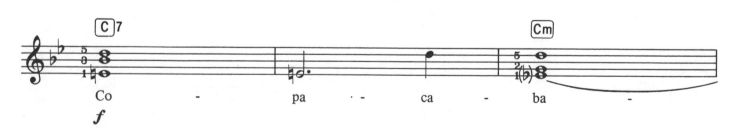

Co - pa - ca - ba -

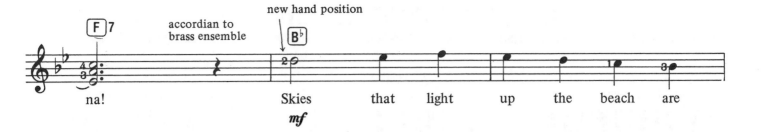

na!   *mf*   Skies   that   light   up   the   beach   are

blu - er   than   blue.   And   an - y

girl   will   teach   the   sam - ba   to   you.

Hey,   sen - or,   you   too,   mad - am,   wan - na   know   where
mp   *cresc.*

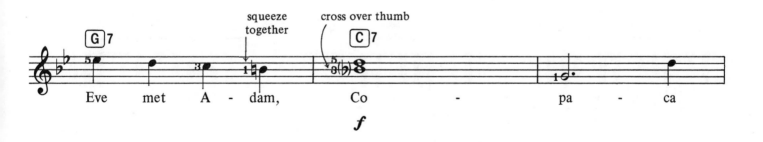

Eve   met   A - dam,   Co   -   pa   -   ca
f

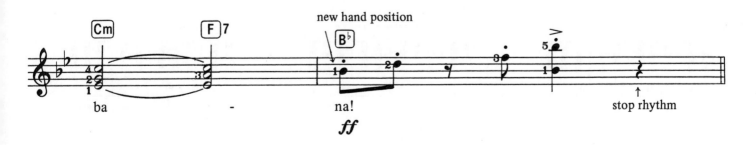

ba   -   na!
ff

MASTER CHORD CHART

C
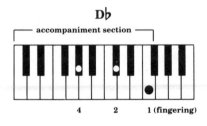

Cm
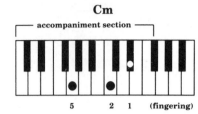

C7
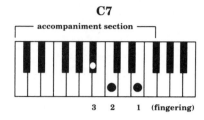

D♭
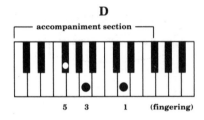

C♯m
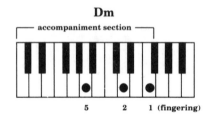

D♭(C♯)7
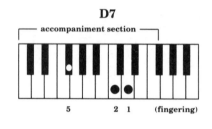

D
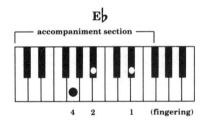

Dm
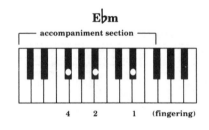

D7
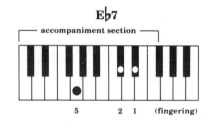

E♭
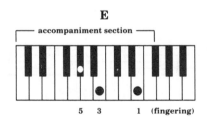

E♭m
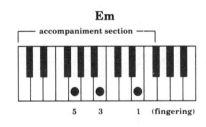

E♭7
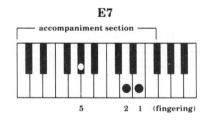

E
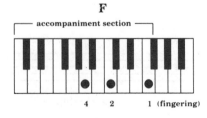

Em
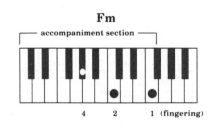

E7
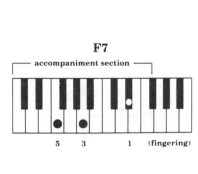

F

Fm

F7

MASTER CHORD CHART

G♭(F♯)

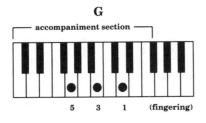

5   3   1   (fingering)

F♯m

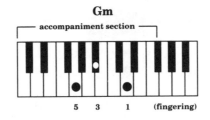

5   3   1   (fingering)

G♭(F♯)7

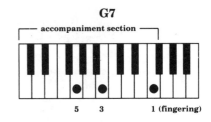

5   3   1   (fingering)

G

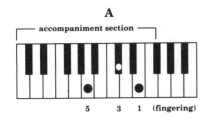

5   3   1   (fingering)

Gm

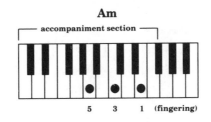

5   3   1   (fingering)

G7

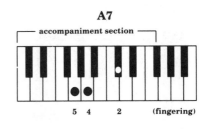

5   3   1 (fingering)

A♭

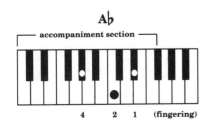

4   2   1   (fingering)

A♭m

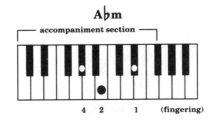

4   2   1   (fingering)

A♭7

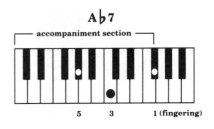

5   3   1 (fingering)

A

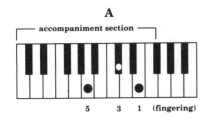

5   3   1 (fingering)

Am

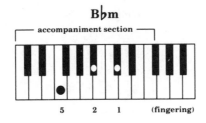

5   3   1   (fingering)

A7

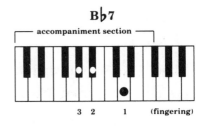

5 4   2   (fingering)

B♭

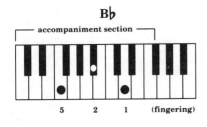

5   2   1   (fingering)

B♭m

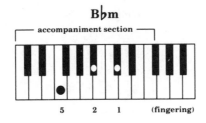

5   2   1   (fingering)

B♭7

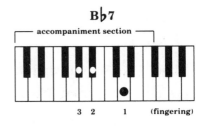

3 2   1   (fingering)

B

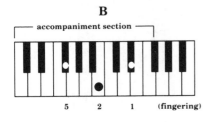

5   2   1   (fingering)

Bm

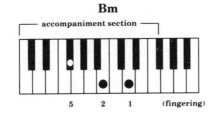

5   2   1   (fingering)

B7

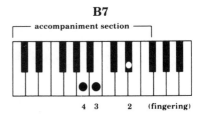

4   3   2   (fingering)

Printed and bound in Great Britain by
Caligraving Limited Thetford Norfolk

9/03 (48753)